THE STORY OF THE DETROIT PISTONS

THE NBA:
A HISTORY
OF HOOPS

THE STORY OF THE
DETROIT
PISTONS

JIM WHITING

CREATIVE EDUCATION

Published by Creative Education
P.O. Box 227, Mankato, Minnesota 56002
Creative Education is an imprint of The Creative Company
www.thecreativecompany.us

Design and production by Blue Design
Art direction by Rita Marshall
Printed in the United States of America

Photographs by Corbis (Bettmann), Getty Images (Glen
Allison, Andrew D. Bernstein/NBAE, Scott Cunningham/
NBAE, Allen Einstein/NBAE, Focus on Sport, George
Gojkovich, Andy Hayt/NBAE, Glenn James/NBAE,
David E. Klutho/Sports Illustrated, George Long/Sports
Illustrated, Melissa Majchrzak/NBAE, Manny Millan/Sports
Illustrated, NBA Photos/NBAE, Dick Raphael/NBAE,
Ezra O. Shaw/Allsport, Jerry Wachter/Sports Illustrated),
Newscom (CURTIS COMPTON/MCT, Chris Szagola/Cal
Sport Media)

Copyright © 2015 Creative Education

International copyright reserved in all countries. No part
of this book may be reproduced in any form without
written permission from the publisher.

Library of Congress Cataloging-in-Publication Data
Whiting, Jim.
The story of the Detroit Pistons / Jim Whiting.
p. cm. — (The NBA: a history of hoops)
Includes index.
Summary: An informative narration of the Detroit Pistons
professional basketball team's history from its 1941
founding in Fort Wayne, Indiana, to today, spotlighting
memorable players and events.
ISBN 978-1-60818-429-3
1. Detroit Pistons (Basketball team)—History—Juvenile
literature. I. Title.

GV885.52.D47W55 2014
796.323'640977434—dc23   2013037448

CCSS: RI.5.1, 2, 3, 8; RH.6-8.4, 5, 7

First Edition
9 8 7 6 5 4 3 2 1

Cover: Guard Brandon Jennings
Page 2: Guard/forward Richard Hamilton
Pages 4-5: Guard Gene Shue (#21)
Page 6: Forward Grant Hill

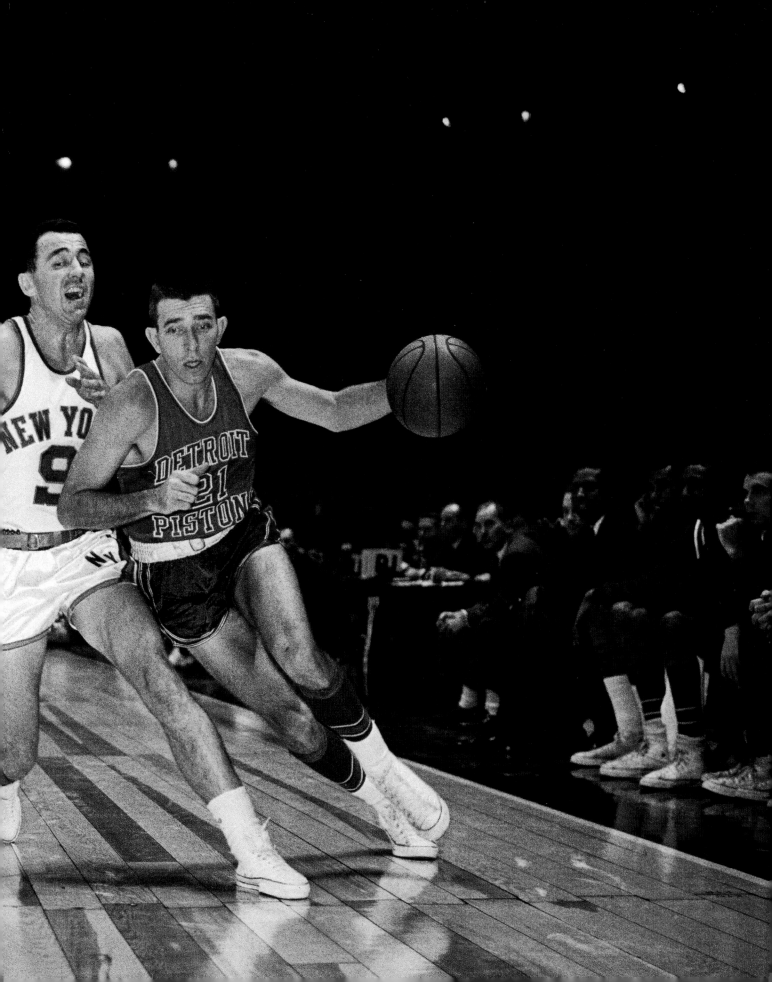

TABLE OF CONTENTS

COURTSIDE STORIES

INTRODUCING...

FROM THE HOOSIER STATE TO MOTOWN

AT DUSK, DETROIT'S CITY LIGHTS GLOW ALONG THE SHORES OF THE DETROIT RIVER.

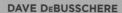

Few American cities are as closely identified with a particular industry as Detroit is with automobile manufacturing. Henry Ford built the first factory there in 1899, and within a few years, some of the nation's best-known brands had made the city their home. Many were named for men who played a key role in their growth and development: railroad mechanic Walter Chrysler, engine developer David Dunbar Buick, Swiss race car driver Louis Chevrolet, and French army officer Antoine Laumet de La Mothe, sieur de Cadillac, who founded Detroit in 1701.

The industry quickly spread beyond Detroit to surrounding communities, many of which made vital components for the cars and were also named for their founders. Pistons, which move up and down in the engine blocks to deliver the power that propels vehicles, were made by Zollner Machine Works in Fort Wayne, Indiana.

AS A DETROIT NATIVE, FORWARD DAVE DeBUSSCHERE (#22) BECAME A HOMETOWN FAVORITE.

The company was founded by Theodore Zollner in 1912, and Zollner's son Fred took over as president in 1945 when his father retired. The sports-loving Fred had already assembled a national champion softball team during the 1930s. Then in 1941, he launched the Fort Wayne Zollner Pistons, a member of the National Basketball League (NBL). Before its move to Detroit 16 years later, the Pistons team would become an accepted institution in Fort Wayne. As writer Gerald Astor recorded, "on the payroll of the Zollner Machine Works are 10 long, loose-limbed fellows who, on the surface of the matter, have little to do with the design,

development and manufacture of pistons. These men do operate, however—and mighty effectively—as the Zollner Machine Works' basketball division."

"Z," as Zollner was nicknamed, personally scouted his players and took a hands-on approach with them. He also ensured that they received the highest pay in the league. The Pistons quickly became the NBL's top team, racking up a 101–32 record on their way to four straight division titles (1943 to 1946) and two league championships (1944 and 1945).

The Pistons' first star was guard Bob McDermott, the team's leading scorer in each

THE FLYING Z

In 1952, general manager Carl Bennett suggested flying the team back and forth to away games, instead of taking the train. Train travel involved frequent overnight runs in sleeping cars with beds too short for the tall players to stretch out. They were exhausted for games the next day. Flying allowed them to return home and get a good night's sleep in their own beds. Because of the uncertainty of chartering a plane, Zollner decided to buy one so that it would always be available. The DC-3 he purchased was fondly dubbed "The Flying Z" and was outfitted with comfortable furniture, a well-stocked bar, a galley, and several four-man tables where the players and coaches could play cards. The plane made the Pistons the envy of their opponents and rival owners. As author Rodger Nelson notes, "Every player asked about the Flying Z had an enthusiastic response." Bennett, however, recalled that Zollner saw the plane differently. "The funny thing about the plane was that Fred was not a flier," he said. "I mean, he was a real 'white-knuckler' when it came to flying."

RODUCING...

AVE
ING

TION GUARD
HT 6-FOOT-3
NS SEASONS
1966–75

When Dave Bing arrived in Detroit in 1966, he was billed as a basketball savior, but fans were skeptical. After all, Bing was the consolation prize in a draft-day coin-flip loss to the New York Knicks that determined which team selected first. But after earning Rookie of the Year honors and then averaging 27.1 points per game the following season, Bing became a sensation. When he retired from basketball, Bing founded a company that supplied steel to the auto industry—and created the perfect metaphor for his career in the process. Bing was as tough as steel, especially in 1972, when he overcame a career-threatening detached retina that required six hours of surgery. "I went 12 hours without sight," Bing said. "My wife and a friend had to lead me around by the hand." Bing's eyesight never fully recovered, and he had to identify his teammates by their size and uniform. In 1974, he was awarded the NBA's Maurice Stokes Award for his tenacity. Bing remained one of the team's steeliest players, missing only four games over his final three seasons in Detroit. In 2009, he was elected mayor of the city.

> ## "I FEEL A CLUB CAN DO BETTER IN A METROPOLITAN AREA OF 2 MILLION PEOPLE THAN AN AREA OF 200,000."
>
> — FRED ZOLLNER ON MOVING THE TEAM TO DETROIT

of its first five seasons, who also acted as coach. In 1945, after he helped the Pistons rally from a two-games-to-none deficit to beat the Sheboygan Redskins in three straight games and win the championship series, NBL coaches voted McDermott the best player in the history of the league.

In 1948, the Pistons and three other NBL teams were absorbed into the Basketball Association of America (BAA). A year later, the NBL and BAA merged to form the National Basketball Association (NBA). Zollner played a key role in brokering the league merger, which, according to legend, took place at his kitchen table. He also helped underwrite the league financially in its first years when it struggled to make ends meet. The league shift didn't do the Pistons any favors, though. From 1949 to 1954, Fort Wayne finished no higher than third in its division and never made it past the second round of the playoffs. But the Pistons made history on November 22, 1950, defeating the Minneapolis Lakers 19–18 in the lowest-scoring NBA game ever.

In 1954, Zollner became the first—and still only—owner to hire a former referee as head coach, picking Charley Eckman to guide a

talented team led by star forward George Yardley and center Larry Foust. In Eckman's first season, the Pistons won the Western Division with a 43–29 record. But they lost to the Syracuse Nationals in the NBA Finals, blowing a 17-point lead in Game 7 and losing by a single point. The Pistons returned to the Finals in 1956 but were beaten 4–1 by the Philadelphia Warriors. By 1957, Zollner didn't think that the Pistons could compete in Fort Wayne and moved the club to Detroit. "I feel a club can do better in a metropolitan area of 2 million people than an area of 200,000," he said.

It was far from Detroit's first foray into pro hoops. Several teams represented the city in a variety of leagues before World War II, in addition to a number of independents. The NBL's Detroit Eagles was the most distinguished among them, providing the pre-Pistons highlight by winning the 1941 World Professional Basketball Tournament. But the team folded when most of its members joined the military. A pair of Detroit teams played professionally in 1946–47: the Falcons of the Basketball Association of America (BAA), which folded after posting a 20–40 mark, and the Gems of the rival NBL, which went 4–40 but moved

"WE FEEL [BOB] FERRY, BAILEY HOWELL, AND [TOP DRAFT PICK] JACKIE MORELAND WILL GIVE US ONE OF THE YOUNGEST AND MOST PROMISING FRONT LINES IN NBA HISTORY."

— GENERAL MANAGER NICK KERBAWY ON THE 1960–61 SEASON

to Minneapolis and morphed into the storied Lakers franchise. Motown's last pro hoops hurrah until the Pistons arrived was the Detroit Vagabond Kings. That team went a dismal 2–17 before moving to Dayton, where, after making some roster changes, it made history as the Rens—the first-ever all-black professional basketball team.

ckman didn't last long after the move. When the Pistons started 9–16, Zollner replaced him with former center/forward Ephraim "Red" Rocha. Rocha bolstered the team with some solid talent by trading with the New York Knicks for veterans such as forward Harry Gallatin, center Nat "Sweetwater" Clifton, and guard Dick McGuire. The best deal, however, was the acquisition of seven-foot center Walter Dukes, a former Harlem Globetrotter who came to the Pistons in an early-season trade. Dukes would play 6 seasons in Detroit and retire in 1963 as the team's all-time rebounding king with 4,986 boards.

In 1959–60, McGuire was elevated to player/coach status. Rookie forward Bailey Howell joined a loaded roster that won seven of nine

games early in the season but eventually ran out of gas. The temporary surge did foreshadow coming success, though. Guard Gene Shue emerged as the team's scoring leader, making the All-Star team, an honor that also went to Dukes and guard Chuck Noble.

Before the 1960–61 season, general manager Nick Kerbawy assessed the team's chances. "We feel [Bob] Ferry, Bailey Howell, and [top pick] Jackie Moreland will give us one of the youngest and most promising front lines in NBA history," Kerbawy declared. Howell turned in an impressive season, but the Pistons sputtered and finished just one game out of the Western Division cellar.

INTRODUCING...

BOB LANIER

POSITION CENTER
HEIGHT 6-FOOT-11
PISTONS SEASONS
1970–80

Bob Lanier began his professional basketball career while he was literally lying flat on his back. The Pistons considered Lanier so good that they signed him to a contract even though he was laid up on a hospital bed recovering from knee surgery. He had injured himself while playing in the 1970 college national tournament for St. Bonaventure University. Lanier possessed a deadly combination of skill and strength. He also happened to have huge feet. His size-22 basketball shoes were the biggest in the league at the time. They were so unique that the Basketball Hall of Fame still features an exhibit where visitors can compare their shoe size with Lanier's. Despite his imposing size, Lanier had a gentle nature. "I think Bob is a very genuine, caring, sensitive, big man," said Joe Dumars, who played guard for Detroit. "He's a big man who seems to have a tremendously big heart. He's not just saying things in front of the camera." After his playing days ended in 1984, Lanier went on to work with the NBA's Read to Achieve program.

PUTTING THE PIECES TOGETHER

AVERAGING 26.5 POINTS A GAME, DYNAMIC FORWARD KELLY TRIPUCKA HAD A SOFT TOUCH.

Even though the Pistons had made it to the playoffs every year since moving to Detroit, they had not won a series since their first postseason in Michigan. But a move into Cobo Arena for the 1961–62 season got the Pistons pumping again. They dispatched the Cincinnati Royals in the first round of the Western Division playoffs and then went head-to-head with the Los Angeles Lakers in the second round. The two teams battled in a series filled with shifts in momentum, but Detroit couldn't keep up and eventually fell in six games.

Coach Charles Wolf took over in 1963–64, and the team limped to 23–57. Things got worse when the Pistons opened the next season 2–9. Forward Dave DeBusschere took over as player/coach. At the age of 24, DeBusschere became the youngest coach in league history. But he, too, seemed powerless to make his team better, and Detroit

INTRODUCING...

CHUCK DALY

COACH
PISTONS SEASONS
1983–92

Ever since his childhood in Pennsylvania, Chuck Daly loved everything about basketball. He never forgot the white leather basketball he and his brother Bud received when Chuck was 12. "When you don't have much materially in life and suddenly you own such a treasure, you think you've died and gone to heaven," Daly said. "I couldn't believe it. Nobody in the world had a white basketball except the Daly brothers." Such appreciation helped Daly bring an intense passion to his teams, especially to Detroit's champion "Bad Boys" crew. "Chuck Daly was the perfect coach for us," guard Isiah Thomas said. "He realized this team was something special, and it seemed as if he pressed the right buttons." Pressing buttons became a Pistons trademark, as Daly's squads played aggressively and often angered opponents. Chicago Bulls star Michael Jordan called them the "dirtiest team in basketball." But Daly knew he coached a special team. "Teams win championships, not individuals," he said. "The players must have ability, ... but they have to be unselfish, and it's hard to find unselfish players." He died in 2009.

dropped to 22–58 in his first full season as coach. Finally, in 1966–67, with the Pistons mired in last place and only eight games remaining, DeBusschere was replaced by assistant coach Donnis "Donnie" Butcher.

A ble to concentrate solely on playing, DeBusschere worked with guard Dave Bing to bring the team new hope. In Bing's first season (1966–67), he had scored 20 points per game and earned the NBA Rookie of the Year award. "You can't open up a man's chest and look at his heart, but I guarantee there's one big [heart] beating in Bing," said legendary Boston Celtics coach Red Auerbach. "Give me one man like Dave Bing, and I'll build a championship team around him." Unfortunately, the Pistons couldn't do that. Detroit made the 1968 playoffs but struggled the next year when DeBusschere was traded.

With the first pick in the 1970 NBA Draft, Detroit selected center Bob Lanier. At 6-foot-11 and a muscular 250 pounds, Lanier was a powerful specimen. "I was well aware of Bob's great strength," said Cleveland Cavaliers center Steve Patterson after battling Lanier for a rebound. "I hammered him, and I practically hung on him. Then, all of a sudden, … he just wrapped his arm around me and threw me to the ground like I was made of straw … I still don't know how he did it."

Lanier briefly revived the Pistons. In 1973–74, under new coach Ray Scott, Detroit jumped to a 52–30 mark and made the playoffs for the first of four straight seasons. But the team could not sustain the success, and those would be the Pistons' last good seasons for a long time. In 1974, Zollner sold the club to entrepreneur

William Davidson with assurances that the Pistons would remain in their home state of Michigan forever. Then, in 1975, the team traded Bing to the Washington Bullets.

In 1978, the Pistons became part of the Eastern Conference and were placed in the Central Division. Lanier was traded to the Milwaukee Bucks in the middle of the 1979–80 season. Without the big center in the middle, Detroit plunged to 16–66 and was in desperate need of a hero.

That hero arrived via the second overall pick in the 1981 NBA Draft: point guard Isiah Thomas, who had just led Indiana University to the national collegiate championship. "I believe God made people to perform certain acts," said Will Robinson, Detroit's assistant general manager. "Frank Sinatra was made to sing, Jesse Owens was made to run, and Isiah Thomas was made to play basketball."

Another 1981 draft pick, Kelly Tripucka, was a high-scoring forward from the University of Notre Dame who also showed promise. During the 1981–82 season, the Pistons traded to obtain veteran guard Vinnie Johnson, an effective outside shooter but also strong enough to muscle his way past bigger players on the inside. Late that season, Detroit traded for tough-guy center Bill Laimbeer. And finally, the Pistons hired Chuck Daly as head coach in 1983. The championship pieces were starting to fall into place.

COURTSIDE STORIES
THE BIRD

By all accounts, forward George "Bird" Yardley didn't seem to have the makings of a star basketball player. But looks can be deceiving. Despite his gangly appearance, he was one of the top players of his era. One of six holdovers from the Fort Wayne squad in 1957, he became Detroit's first team captain. That year, the jump-shot pioneer set the team single-game scoring record with 52 points against the Syracuse Nationals. In the regular-season finale, Yardley foiled Syracuse's triple-teaming tactics and his final basket gave him 2,001 points for the season—making him the first player to surpass the 2,000 mark. "I've been around basketball just about all my life, and I've yet to see a jump shot better than Yardley's," Pistons coach Charley Eckman said. Yardley agreed. "There might have been others who were good jumpers, but I could move my body well to either side while in the air and still control my shot," he explained. Yardley's Pistons career ended in 1959 after an argument with owner Fred Zollner. He was traded to the Syracuse Nationals with 15 games remaining in the season.

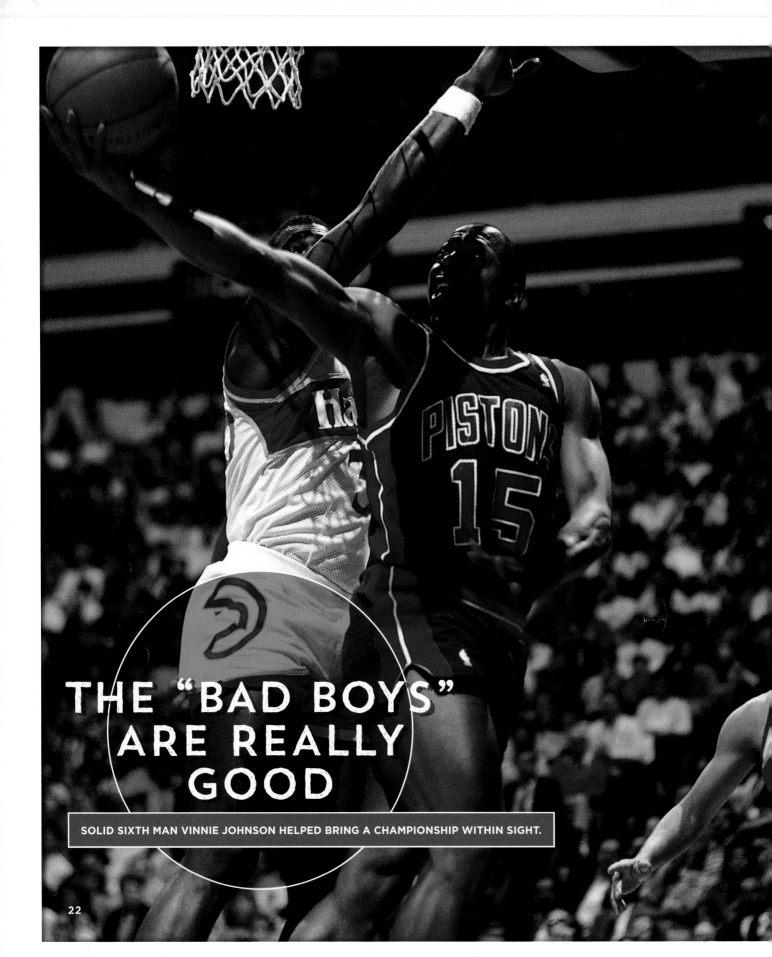

THE "BAD BOYS" ARE REALLY GOOD

SOLID SIXTH MAN VINNIE JOHNSON HELPED BRING A CHAMPIONSHIP WITHIN SIGHT.

Detroit's play improved quickly, and the Pistons made it to the second round of the 1985 Eastern Conference playoffs against the Boston Celtics. In Game 4, Johnson earned a lasting nickname after scoring 22 fourth-quarter points in a 102–99 win to tie the series. Celtics guard Danny Ainge remarked, "If that guy in Chicago [football player William Perry] is 'The Refrigerator,' then Vinnie Johnson is 'The Microwave.' He sure heated up in a hurry." But Boston bested Detroit in each of the remaining two games.

In 1985, more pieces of the Pistons' rebuilding project fell into place. In the NBA Draft that year, they selected a little-known guard from McNeese State University named Joe Dumars. The team also traded with the Bullets for forwards Rick Mahorn and Mike Gibson. The next year, Detroit drafted 6-foot-11 center John Salley from the Georgia

INTENSE PRESSURE

During the 1980s, when the Detroit Pistons were known as the "Bad Boys," center Bill Laimbeer was considered the baddest of all. He threw elbows, fists, and hips into his opponents and probably earned more boos and vile nicknames from opposing fans than anyone in the history of the NBA. Opposing players often retaliated with punches, for, as Boston Celtics forward Larry Bird once said, "We don't like him that good." Eventually, the Chicago Bulls decided to get to the bottom of Laimbeer's tactics. They trained a camera on him throughout the 1991 playoffs to see what he was doing. What they discovered was amazing—Laimbeer often grabbed players at their pressure points (such as on the biceps or a nerve on the forearm) to deaden their arms. Chicago formally complained to the league, but no action was taken. Through it all, Laimbeer was a four-time All-Star who helped the Pistons win a pair of championships. He also became the 19th player in NBA history to collect more than 10,000 career points (with 13,790) and 10,000 rebounds (with 10,400).

BILL LAIMBEER

Institute of Technology and Dennis Rodman, a wily forward from tiny Southeastern Oklahoma State University. Before the 1986–87 season began, the team added another impressive player when it shipped Tripucka for Adrian Dantley, one of the best-scoring small forwards and toughest low-post threats in the league. Detroit was now loaded with talent.

Coach Daly preached an aggressive defense, and the Pistons earned the nickname "Bad Boys" for their physical style of play. Thomas became an incomparable floor general. Dumars and Johnson were an interchangeable rotation at the other guard position. Laimbeer and Mahorn proved to be imposing enforcers and shot blockers in the paint, while Dantley was a nightmare for defenders in the half-court. Salley and Rodman, meanwhile, provided sparks off the bench by disrupting their opponents' rhythms with tough, smothering defense and efficient rebounding. The Pistons soared to a 52–30 mark and reached the 1987 Eastern Conference finals, where they fell to the Celtics.

Detroit stormed back the next season, winning both the division and the conference, something it had not done since the 1950s.

JOHN SALLEY BECAME ONE OF THE PISTONS' BEST ALL-TIME SHOT BLOCKERS, WITH 709 OVER HIS CAREER.

THE WORM TURNS

His difficult childhood and mediocre high school basketball experience convinced Dennis Rodman to give up the sport and work as a night janitor at Dallas-Fort Worth International Airport. But then he had a growth spurt and gave basketball another shot at the college level, becoming a three-time National Association of Intercollegiate Athletics (NAIA) All-American. Drafted by Detroit in 1986, he was a perfect fit with the Pistons and their team of "Bad Boys." He soon acquired the nickname "Worm" for his ability to squirm between players underneath the basket and snag rebounds. He was also a lockdown defender. During his NBA career and afterward, Rodman became notorious for things such as dying his hair a bewildering array of colors; dressing in women's clothing; and for a couple of short-lived, high-profile marriages. He wrestled professionally, acted in movies and television, hosted his own reality talk show, and wrote two books about his life. Despite his wild off-court behavior, Rodman is regarded as one of the NBA's all-time greatest rebounders and defensive players. In 2011, he was inducted into the Naismith Memorial Basketball Hall of Fame.

"DUMARS WOULDN'T MISS. WE KEPT WAITING FOR HIM TO MISS. YOU COULD FEEL THE WHOLE BUILDING WAITING. BUT IT WAS AS IF HE HAD FORGOTTEN HOW."

— MITCH KUPCHAK ON JOE DUMARS'S MVP PERFORMANCE

In the six-game conference finals, the Pistons demolished the Celtics. At long last, Detroit was in the NBA Finals. Although the Pistons lost to the Lakers in seven hard-fought games, they would not be denied the next season.

In 1988–89, the team moved into a new arena, The Palace of Auburn Hills. That season, the Pistons dominated the league with a 63–19 record and pounded their way through the playoffs to meet the Lakers again in the Finals. This rematch was no contest as Detroit swept L.A. in four games. Dumars exploded for an average of 27.3 points per game during the series and was named Finals Most Valuable Player (MVP). "Dumars wouldn't miss," said Mitch Kupchak, a Lakers team official. "We kept waiting for him to miss. You could feel the whole building waiting. But it was as if he had forgotten how."

The Pistons roared to a third consecutive division title the next season and again reached the Finals, where they battled the Portland Trail Blazers. The five-game series turned out to be a lopsided affair, with Portland's sole victory coming in overtime of Game 2. Thomas was masterful. To observers, it seemed he was all over the court, making shot after shot and doing a little bit of everything to help the Pistons win.

He was voted Finals MVP after averaging 27.6 points, 7 assists, and 5.2 rebounds. In Game 5, The Microwave lived up to his clutch reputation, nailing the series-winning shot with 0.7 second left on the clock.

The Pistons were eager to "three-peat." But it was not to be. In the 1991 playoffs, superstar guard Michael Jordan and the Chicago Bulls—whom the Pistons had repeatedly beaten in previous years' playoffs—won the conference, supplanting Detroit as the top Eastern heavyweight. In 1992–93, the Pistons went 40–42 and missed the playoffs for the first time in a decade. Rodman was traded to the San Antonio Spurs, and Laimbeer and Thomas retired. By 1994, only Dumars remained from Detroit's championship era.

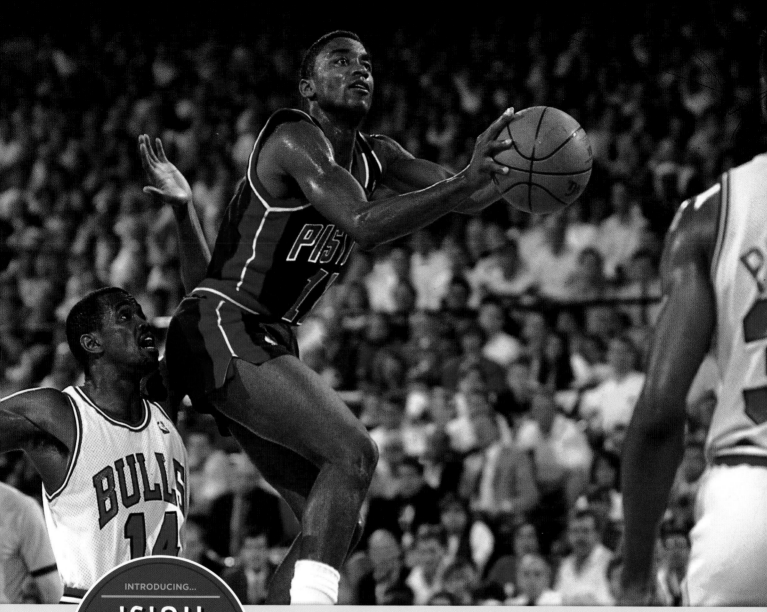

INTRODUCING...

ISIAH THOMAS

POSITION GUARD
HEIGHT 6-FOOT-1
PISTONS SEASONS
1981–94

Isiah "Zeke" Thomas spent his entire playing career in Detroit and was the unquestioned leader of the "Bad Boys." "If I'm just trying to sum Zeke up in a couple of sentences, it's almost impossible to do," teammate Joe Dumars said. "By far, he's the best player I've ever played with." After the Pistons finally broke out of their playoff rut and reached the 1988 NBA Finals, they took a three-games-to-two series lead over the Los Angeles Lakers. But in the third quarter of Game 6, Thomas sprained his ankle. Yet the injury seemed to make him stronger and more determined. He scored 25 points in a single quarter, an NBA Finals record. But Thomas's 43 total points weren't enough, and the Pistons then lost the series when he was unable to contribute much in Game 7. Thomas took the loss to heart and worked even harder to help the Pistons become the league's best team. As a result, Detroit won back-to-back championships. Upon retirement, Thomas entered the executive ranks with the Toronto Raptors and New York Knicks.

BACK TO THE TOP

IN THE 1997–98 SEASON, BISON DELE POSTED A CAREER-HIGH 16.2 POINTS PER GAME.

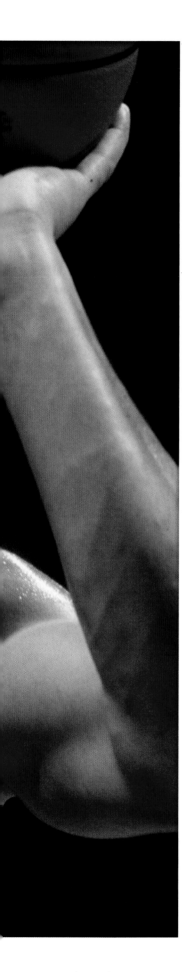

Detroit began rebuilding when it selected forward Grant Hill in the 1994 NBA Draft and paired him with young sharpshooting guard Allan Houston. Although Detroit's record was only 28–54 that year, Hill became the first Pistons player since Dave Bing (in 1967) to be named Rookie of the Year.

Under new coach Doug Collins, the 1995–96 Pistons leapt to 46–36. Although they made the playoffs, they were swept by the Orlando Magic. In 1997, they brought in two key additions, trading for guard/forward Jerry Stackhouse and signing center Brian Williams (who later changed his name to Bison Dele). That year, Hill became the first player since Celtics great Larry Bird (in 1989–90) to average at least 20 points, 9 rebounds, and 7 assists per game in a season (1996–97), an accomplishment that has not been replicated.

BASKET-BRAWL AT THE PALACE

When the Detroit Pistons took on the Indiana Pacers on November 19, 2004, at The Palace of Auburn Hills, the spectators assumed it would be another normal roundball game. But on this night, basketball took a back seat to punching. The problem started with a scuffle between Pistons center Ben Wallace and Pacers forward Ron Artest. Things escalated from there. Officials stopped the game with 45.9 seconds remaining after players from both teams joined in the pushing and shoving. As Artest was resting on the scorer's table after being separated from the fray, a Pistons fan lobbed a drink that struck him. Artest and Pacers forward Stephen Jackson jumped into the crowd, and as other Indiana players joined them, players and fans exchanged punches. Ice, cups, and other debris began raining down onto the court, and a full-on riot ensued. After the brawl, many players were fined and suspended, and some fans were even prosecuted in court on assault charges. Said NBA commissioner David Stern, "The events of the game were shocking, repulsive, and inexcusable, a humiliation for everyone associated with the NBA."

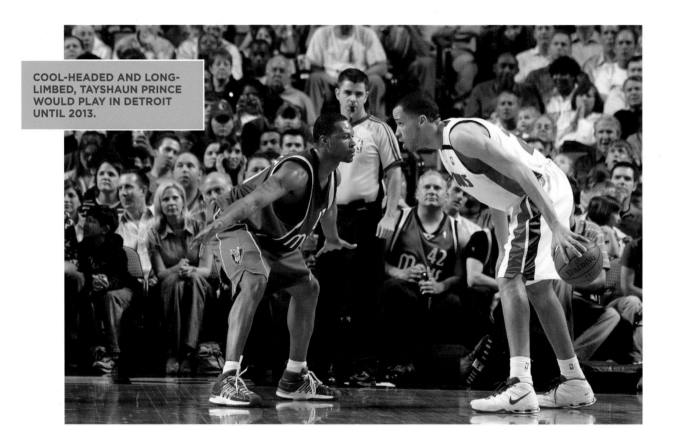

COOL-HEADED AND LONG-LIMBED, TAYSHAUN PRINCE WOULD PLAY IN DETROIT UNTIL 2013.

Dumars finally retired in 1999 and became team president. He left a huge hole in the lineup, and the team struggled for wins. Despite Hill's statistical supremacy, Detroit never advanced far in the playoffs. So, in 2000, when Hill opted to become a free agent, the Pistons organized a sign-and-trade deal with Orlando. In return for Hill, they received guard Chucky Atkins and Ben Wallace, an intimidating 6-foot-9 center with rippling muscles and a fuzzy Afro, who would go on to become a four-time NBA Defensive Player of the Year.

Rick Carlisle was named head coach in 2001 and jump-started the Pistons. In two seasons under Carlisle, Detroit finished 50–32 and charged deep into the playoffs. In 2002, the Pistons traded for smooth-scoring guard Richard Hamilton, who worked alongside do-it-all rookie forward Tayshaun Prince. Though he had brought competitive basketball back to Motown, Carlisle was let go in 2003 after the Pistons were swept by the New Jersey Nets in the Eastern Conference finals.

The Pistons then made headlines by signing Hall of Fame coach Larry Brown away from the Philadelphia 76ers. Brown was determined to

INTRODUCING...

JOE DUMARS

POSITION GUARD
HEIGHT 6-FOOT-3
PISTONS SEASONS
1985–99

Even though many Detroit fans had never heard of Joe Dumars when he was drafted, his hardworking style of play quickly endeared him to the Pistons faithful. Dumars was considered one of the greatest competitors in the league and was so widely respected that he was awarded the inaugural NBA Sportsmanship Award in 1996. Thereafter, the league even named the award's trophy after him. By the time his playing days ended in 1999, Dumars had become the team's leading three-point shooter, with 990 made, and its second-leading scorer, with 16,401 career points. "Throughout his 14-year career, Joe carried himself with dignity and integrity and showed that one can be both a great athlete and a great sportsman," league deputy commissioner Russ Granik said on the occasion of Dumars's retirement. The Pistons didn't allow Dumars to go far, though. He was immediately hired as president of Detroit's basketball operations and excelled at that, too. As the architect of Detroit's remarkable two-year turnaround in 2001 and 2002, he was named by *The Sporting News* as NBA Executive of the Year in 2003.

WHEN TOWERING "BIG BEN" WALLACE SCORED, FANS SET OFF A LOUD CLOCK CHIME IN THE ARENA.

36

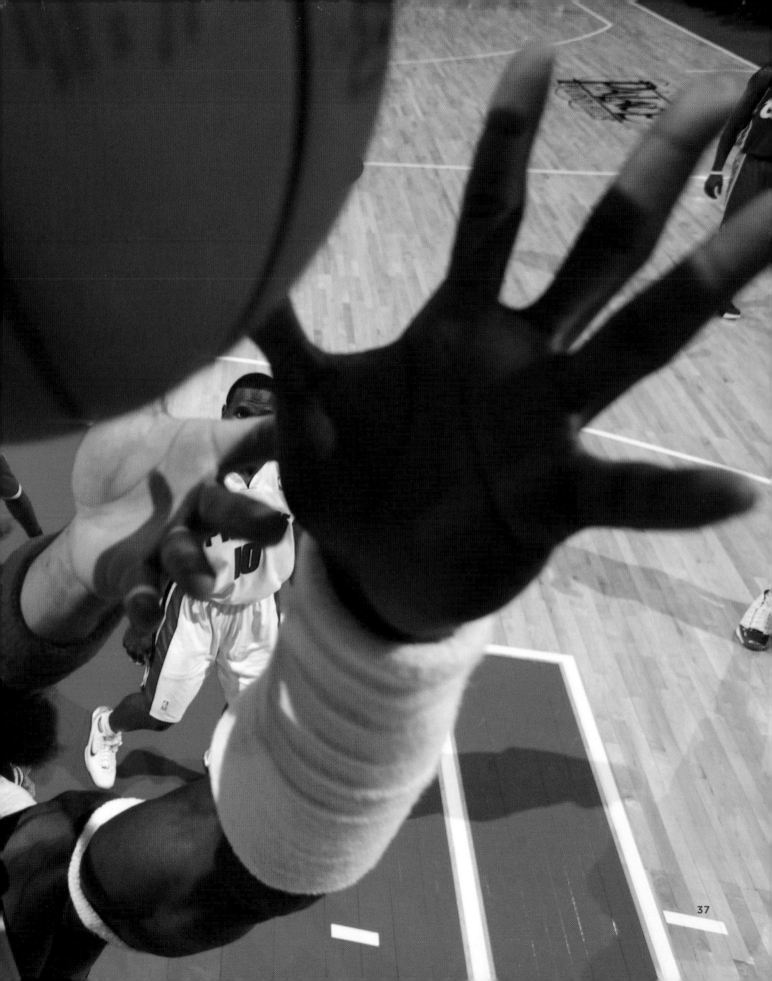

LACKING IN LONG-RANGE ABILITY, RODNEY STUCKEY USED HIS SIZE TO DRIVE INSIDE.

"WE SAID TO OURSELVES, 'ANYTHING IS POSSIBLE IF YOU PLAY TOGETHER AS FIVE, NOT JUST ON THE OFFENSIVE END BUT ON THE DEFENSIVE END, TOO.'"

— RICHARD HAMILTON ON THE 2003 NBA FINALS

make Detroit a winner again. "I saw a team with a chance to win, a team with quality ownership in Mr. [William] Davidson and quality leadership with a guy like Joe [Dumars], a team with character guys," Brown said.

A late-season trade for power forward Rasheed Wallace kicked Hamilton, Ben Wallace, point guard Chauncey Billups, and the rest of the team into high gear. Detroit finished 54–28 and raced through the playoffs to meet the Lakers in the NBA Finals. Ben Wallace considered reaching the Finals his finest honor of all. "Yeah, [winning awards] means a lot, but it is not something I am going to hang my hat on," he said. "Getting back to the Finals is our main focus."

The star-laden Lakers had recently won three consecutive NBA championships. But the Pistons shocked the sports world by beating the Lakers four games to one for the franchise's third league championship. "We didn't worry about what people wrote in the papers or what people were saying on TV," said Hamilton. "We said to ourselves, 'Anything is possible if you play together as five, not just on the offensive end but on the defensive end, too.'"

In 2004–05, the Pistons nearly pulled off a repeat, making it all the way to the Finals before getting ousted by the Spurs in seven games. Detroit seemed destined for another Finals appearance the following year after barreling to a franchise-best 64–18 record under new coach Flip Saunders. But the team fell apart in the conference finals and lost to the Miami Heat. Still, the Pistons had accomplished much in just a few seasons. "We got to the Finals twice and won it once," said Billups. "I think that is a great run."

Detroit remained formidable over the next few seasons as it marched to the Eastern Conference finals twice more. In 2007, the Pistons lost in the conference finals to forward LeBron James and his upstart crew of Cleveland Cavaliers. And in 2007–08, Detroit got some spark from young-gun players such as guard Rodney Stuckey, but the team lost out to the Celtics in the conference finals. In 2008–09, the Pistons made a move that damaged the team's chemistry, trading Billups to the Denver Nuggets for veteran guard Allen Iverson. Detroit barely made the playoffs as a number 8 seed

POINT GUARD WILL BYNUM HONED HIS GAME IN ISRAEL BEFORE JOINING THE PISTONS IN 2008.

and was swept by the Cavaliers. Iverson left the team soon afterward.

The Pistons missed the playoffs for the first time in nine years in the 2009–10 season, finishing 27–55 and in last place in the Central Division. They showed little improvement the following year, winning only three more games to finish 30–52. Yet another member of the 2004 championship team, Richard Hamilton,

left Detroit, and the Pistons were seemingly in full rebuilding mode with Stuckey, young forward Jonas Jerebko, and their top choice in the 2011 NBA Draft, guard Brandon Knight of the University of Kentucky. After a horrendous 4–20 start to the lockout-shortened 2011–12 season, Detroit played .500 ball the rest of the way to finish 25–41 and raise hopes for the future. The Pistons added 6-foot-10 University

INTRODUCING...

RICHARD HAMILTON

**POSITION GUARD / FORWARD
HEIGHT 6-FOOT-6
PISTONS SEASONS
2002–11**

As a high-schooler in the mining town of Coatesville, Pennsylvania, Richard Hamilton developed into a local basketball legend. Although he did not make the varsity team his freshman year, he did catch the eye of coach Ricky Hicks, who took him under his wing. Hamilton met with Hicks most mornings at six o'clock to work on his game. Hicks also taught him a unique breathing technique that provided better stamina. It was around this time that Hamilton first learned of another basketball phenom from eastern Pennsylvania named Kobe Bryant. During a three-on-three tournament in Philadelphia, Bryant's father, Joe, was watching the action and noticed Hamilton, who was the only other player who could keep up with his son. Hamilton and Bryant would face off throughout high school and even play together on state all-star teams. Once he reached the pros, "Rip" solidified his status as one of the league's most talented stars, exhibiting a sweet midrange jumper on offense and playing relentless defense on the other end. Hamilton distinguished himself as the Pistons' clear leader in the mid-2000s.

RASHEED WALLACE (CENTER) LOOKED TO RALLY HIS TEAMMATES FOR A NEEDED WIN.

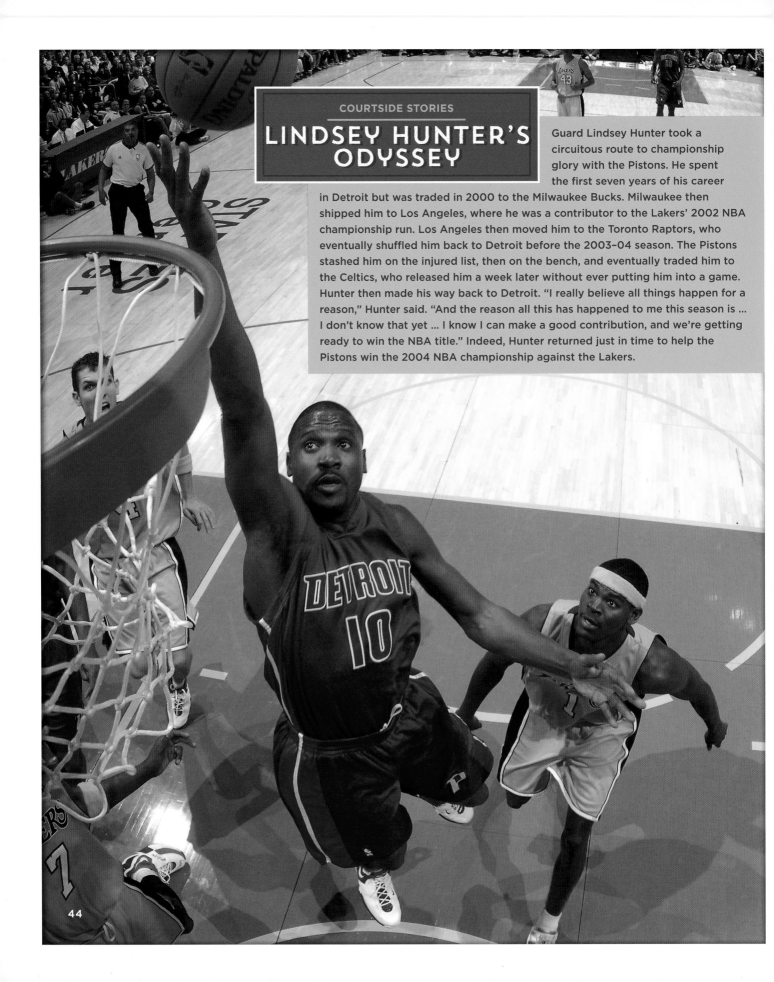

LINDSEY HUNTER'S ODYSSEY

Guard Lindsey Hunter took a circuitous route to championship glory with the Pistons. He spent the first seven years of his career in Detroit but was traded in 2000 to the Milwaukee Bucks. Milwaukee then shipped him to Los Angeles, where he was a contributor to the Lakers' 2002 NBA championship run. Los Angeles then moved him to the Toronto Raptors, who eventually shuffled him back to Detroit before the 2003–04 season. The Pistons stashed him on the injured list, then on the bench, and eventually traded him to the Celtics, who released him a week later without ever putting him into a game. Hunter then made his way back to Detroit. "I really believe all things happen for a reason," Hunter said. "And the reason all this has happened to me this season is … I don't know that yet … I know I can make a good contribution, and we're getting ready to win the NBA title." Indeed, Hunter returned just in time to help the Pistons win the 2004 NBA championship against the Lakers.

"WHAT IS SO IMPRESSIVE FOR THIS BIG MAN IS
HOW HE CAN PASS THE BALL IN A HIGH-LOW
SETTING OR WITH HIS BACK TO THE BASKET."
— ESPN ANALYSTS ON ANDRE DRUMMOND

of Connecticut center Andre Drummond with their first pick in the 2012 Draft. "What is so impressive for this big man is how he can pass the ball in a high-low setting or with his back to the basket," commented Paul Biancardi and Adam Finkelstein of ESPN. "Plus, he can defend in the low or high post."

espite missing more than a month with a back injury, Drummond proved to be effective in relatively limited action. "Detroit Pistons big man Andre Drummond was one of the most impressive rookies in the NBA this season, a dynamic force who managed many impressive stat lines despite playing only 20.7 minutes per game," wrote Yahoo Sports basketball columnist Eric Freeman. "There are good reasons to be bullish about his future." On the team level, the Pistons' 29–53 record in 2012–13 did not seem particularly heartening. But as Mike Payne of DetroitBadBoys.com noted, "this season was a moral success in that the team finally severed its last remaining connection to the 2004 title team. It's no longer grasping at the past; it

has embraced its own future."

Detroit aimed to assemble a playoff contender for the 2013–14 season, adding high-scoring forward Josh Smith and smooth-dishing guard Brandon Jennings to the lineup. But the team couldn't manage to cobble together a decent record, leading to a midseason coaching change as assistant coach John Loyer became the head man. Pistons fans wondered what it would take to restore their team to glory.

In an automobile engine, pistons are constantly in motion: up and down, up and down, up and down. In the NBA, the Pistons have done the same thing. Their ups have produced championships, and their downs have dropped them toward the league's basement. While recent years have trended downward, the Detroit faithful are optimistic that their team will again head upward and contend for more titles in the seasons to come.

EVEN TRIPLE-TEAMING WASN'T ENOUGH TO STOP ANDRE DRUMMOND FROM CONNECTING.

47

INDEX